Fruit Gems

A Collection of *Fruit Recipes*

by
Bella McAdams

TEACH Services, Inc.
P U B L I S H I N G
www.TEACHServices.com • (800) 367-1844

World rights reserved. This book or any portion thereof may not be copied or reproduced in any form or manner whatever, except as provided by law, without the written permission of the publisher, except by a reviewer who may quote brief passages in a review.

The author assumes full responsibility for the accuracy of all facts and quotations as cited in this book. The opinions expressed in this book are the author's personal views and interpretations, and do not necessarily reflect those of the publisher.

This book is provided with the understanding that the publisher is not engaged in giving spiritual, legal, medical, or other professional advice. If authoritative advice is needed, the reader should seek the counsel of a competent professional.

Copyright © Bella McAdams
Copyright © 2014 TEACH Services, Inc.
ISBN-13: 978-1-4796-0320-6 (Paperback)
ISBN-13: 978-1-4796-0321-3 (ePub)
ISBN-13: 978-1-4796-0322-0 (Mobi)
Library of Congress Control Number: 2014936221

Published by

www.TEACHServices.com • (800) 367-1844

Table of Contents

Introduction 7

Cakes 9
- Nectarine Pound Cake
- Tropical Cocktail Cake
- Blackberry Cake
- Lemony Nectarine Graham Cake
- Blackberry Lime Pudding Cake
- Mixed Berry Shortcake
- Dinner Plum Cake
- Applesauce Loaf
- Fruit Loaves

Bars & Cookies 17
- Chocolate Chip Pear Bars
- Lemon Lime Bars
- Coconut Macaroon Cookies
- Harvest Cookies

Pies 21
- Fruit Custard Pie
- Pineapple Meringue Pie
- Creamy Raspberry Pie
- Mixed Fruit Pie
- Double Blackberry Pie
- Awesome Banana Cream Pie
- Creamy Blackberry Pie
- Mince Fruit Pie
- Apple Pie Supreme
- Apple Blackberry Cobbler

Puddings & Mousses 29
- Coconut Pudding with Pineapple
- Butterscotch Banana Pudding
- Lime Mousse with Blackberries
- Banana Mousse
- Apricot Whip
- Purple Cow Fondue
- Orange Whip
- Baked Pears & Raspberry Fondue

Soups & Compotes 37
- Festive Apple & Pear Compote
- Wintertime Compote
- Chilled Fruit Stew
- Zesty Peach Soup
- Three Berry Soup

Baked & Broiled Fruit Dishes 44
- Honey Baked Goldies
- Baked Pears
- Sunny Poached Pears
- Oven Baked Fruits
- Broiled Pineapples & Plums
- Microwaved Baked Apples
- Peach Royale
- Apple Fritters
- Apple Harvest Casserole

Breakfast Fruit Treats 51
    Breakfast Fruit Salad
    Breakfast Banana Split
    Hot Apple Granola
    Sundae Fruit Breakfast Delight
    Blueberry Applesauce Muffins

Smoothies, Sorbets, & Drinks 57
    Grape Ice
    Watermelon Slush
    Apricot Bliss
    Peach Refresher
    Raspberry Cocoa Chiller
    Berry Smoothie
    Kiwi Cooler
    Purple Sherbet
    Orange Banana Slush
    Mango & Blueberry Smoothie
    Blueberry Sorbet
    Watermelon Sunset
    Honeydew Sorbet
    Summer Fruit Breeze
    Pineapple Freezie
    Peachy Mint Sorbet
    Summer Citrus Punch
    Party Punch
    Strawberry Milk Punch
    Fruit Punch

Relishes & Salads 69
    Going Green Salad
    Refreshing Kiwi Salad
    Springtime Fruit Salad
    Cranberry Salad
    Creamy Ambrosia Mold
    Pineapple Apricot Salad
    Fruit Salad with Dried Cherries
    Apple Salad with Dates
    Cran-Pear Relish
    Strawberry Orange Relish
    Cranberry Pear Medley

Miscellaneous Desserts & Snacks 77
    Festive Fruit Pizza
    Double Fruit Crisp
    Dinner Dates
    Chocolate Dipped Fruits
    Better-for-you Banana Split
    Banana Bonanza with Strawberries
    Berries with Warm Vanilla Sauce
    Apple-Blueberry Crumble
    Cran-Blue Brownies
    Anytime Banana Muffins
    Coconut Date Balls
    Chill Out Berry Consommé
    Cherry Sweet Dream
    Spicy Raisins
    Summer Soother
    Pineapple & Grapes with Strawberry Sauce
    Little Fruit Gems
    Fruit Truffle
    Ricotta Cream Dessert
    Prunes & Kumquats Combo
    Frozen Fruit Freeze
    Cinnamon Orange Sauce
    Grilled Fruit with Glaze
    Melon Ring
    Fruit Candy Loaf
    Fruit Trio with Topping
    Papaya Dreamer
    Pear Supreme
    Peachy Dreams
    Peach Streusel
    Peach Treat with Sauce

"In the midst of the street of it, and on either side of the river, was there the tree of life, which bare twelve manner of fruits, and yielded her fruit every month: and the leaves of the tree were for the healing of the nations."
Revelation 22:2

Introduction

Do you love fruit? If so, this cookbook contains more than 100 recipes featuring a wide variety of fruits. From salads, smoothies, and pies to cakes, cookies, and puddings, you will find recipes that will delight the palate. Whether you like your fruit raw, baked, chilled, or grilled, you will find recipes to suit your fancy.

For those looking for low fat recipes, you can easily substitute ingredients, for example you may choose to use reduced fat cream cheese instead of regular cream cheese, or low fat milk or soy milk for whole milk. As for eggs, egg whites or egg products may be used instead of whole eggs. Just remember that with any substitution there may be some slight variations in taste and texture.

Some recipes in this book call for gelatin. If you prefer to use vegetarian gelatin, please do so. I was unable to find vegetarian gelatin in the stores in my area, so I did not experiment with that substitute.

Most of the fruit used in these recipes is available year round, which means that finding the right fruit for the recipe you are in the mood for will not be difficult.

When selecting fruit, buy fruit that is in season. Fruit such as peaches and nectarines should not be too hard or too soft or mushy. Fresh fruit that is ripe will have a pleasant fragrance. Canned and frozen fruit is always available and, in most recipes, may be used instead of fresh fruit.

Within this cookbook you will discover reinvented or modified versions of some of your favorite fruit recipes. Enjoy!

Bella

Cakes

Nectarine Pound Cake

1 cup butter
3 cups unbleached all-purpose flour
2 cups nectarines, peeled and diced
2 1/2 cups sugar
6 large eggs
1/2 cup cream
1/2 cup sour cream
1 teaspoon vanilla extract
1/2 teaspoon salt
1/4 teaspoon baking soda

Preheat oven to 350 degrees.

In a large bowl, mix butter and sugar together until smooth and fluffy. Add eggs, one at a time, making sure to mix well; then add vanilla extract. In a second bowl, mix flour, salt, and baking soda together. Pour egg mixture into flour mixture. Add cream and sour cream, and mix until smooth. Gently fold in chopped nectarines.

Pour batter into a nonstick bundt pan. Bake for 1 hour and 15 minutes. Invert onto a serving plate while warm, and serve.

Tropical Cocktail Cake

1 cup unbleached all-purpose flour
    or whole wheat pastry flour
2/3 cup sugar
1 teaspoon baking soda
1/4 teaspoon salt
1 15-ounce can tropical fruit cocktail
    or fruit salad
1 large egg
2 tablespoons canola oil
1 teaspoon coconut flavoring
1 teaspoon vanilla extract

Topping
1/2 cup unsweetened coconut flakes
2 tablespoons packed brown sugar

Preheat oven to 350 degrees. Lightly spray or oil a 9-inch square baking pan.

In a medium bowl, whisk together flour, sugar, baking soda, and salt. In a large bowl, drain syrup from fruit cocktail. Whisk in egg, oil, and vanilla extract. Coarsely chop fruit and stir into juice mixture. Add the dry ingredients to the wet ingredients, and stir to combine. In the same bowl used for the dry ingredients, mix together coconut and brown sugar.

Pour cake batter into the prepared pan, and bake for 20 minutes. Remove cake from the oven, and sprinkle with coconut mixture. Return cake to the oven, and bake for 10 more minutes or until coconut is toasted. Remove from the oven, and let the cake cool in the pan or on a rack. Cut into 9 squares. Serve warm or at room temperature.

Blackberry Cake

1 1/2 cups blackberries
1 cup unbleached all-purpose flour
2/3 cup sugar
1/2 teaspoon baking soda
1/2 teaspoon ground ginger
1/4 teaspoon salt
1/2 cup buttermilk
2 tablespoons canola oil
2 lightly beaten eggs

Preheat oven to 375 degrees. Spray an 8-inch round cake pan with cooking spray.

Set the blackberries aside in a bowl. In a medium bowl, combine flour, sugar, baking soda, ginger, and salt. Make a well in the center, and pour in buttermilk, oil, and eggs. Stir until no dry flour is visible. Pour batter into the prepared pan. Spoon the berries on top, and sprinkle with sugar.

Bake for 35 to 40 minutes or until a toothpick comes out clean. Cool on a wire rack. Transfer the cake from the pan to a plate, and serve.

If you love blackberry pie, try this blackberry cake for a delightful change.

Lemony Nectarine Graham Cake

1/2 cup unsalted butter
1 cup sugar
2 large eggs
1/4 cup dried lemon peel
Zest of 1 lemon
Juice of 1/2 lemon
1 nectarine, peeled and diced
3/4 cup milk
1 teaspoon orange extract
1 teaspoon vanilla extract
2 cups graham cracker crumbs
2/3 cup unbleached all-purpose flour
2 teaspoons baking powder
1/2 teaspoon salt
1/4 teaspoon baking soda

Preheat oven to 350 degrees. Spray an 8-inch round non-stick bundt pan with cooking spray.

Place softened butter in a mixing bowl, and beat in sugar. Add eggs, one at a time, beating well after each addition. Stir in diced lemon peel, lemon zest, and nectarine. Slowly add milk, extracts, and lemon juice. Place graham crumbs in a separate bowl, and stir in salt, baking powder, baking soda, and flour. Fold egg mixture into crumbs until well blended. Pour batter into the prepared pan, smoothing out the top.

Bake for 45 to 50 minutes or until the center of the cake is firm. Remove from the oven and cool in pan. Remove cake from pan and serve..

If nectarines are not available, you can uses peaches.

Makes 10 servings.

Blackberry Lime Pudding Cake

1 tablespoon fresh lime juice
1 teaspoon grated lime peel
2 teaspoons cornstarch
12 ounces frozen blackberries
1 cup sugar
3 eggs
1 cup buttermilk
1/2 teaspoon vanilla extract
1/2 cup unbleached all-purpose flour
1/2 teaspoon baking powder
Pinch salt

Preheat oven to 350 degrees. Lightly oil six ovenproof custard cups. Place the cups in a 2-inch deep baking pan. Begin to heat water to add to the pan just before baking.

In a bowl, combine lime juice with cornstarch and add blackberries and half of the sugar; toss lightly. Separate the egg yolks from the egg whites. In a small bowl, with an electric mixer or a whisk, beat egg whites until stiff. Set aside. In a large bowl, beat egg yolks and buttermilk with remaining sugar. Beat in lime peel, vanilla extract, salt, flour, and baking powder. Gently stir in the blackberry mixture; then fold in the beaten egg whites. Spoon the batter evenly into the prepared cups.

Pour very hot water into the baking pan until the water reaches about halfway up the sides of the cups. Bake for 40 to 50 minutes or until puffed, firm on top, and golden. Refrigerate, and serve chilled.

Mixed Berry Shortcake

4 cups mixed berries
1/2 cup sugar
2 cups unbleached all-purpose flour
1 tablespoon baking powder
1/2 teaspoon salt
1 stick unsalted butter
3/4 cup milk
1 cup heavy cream
3 tablespoons powdered sugar
1/2 teaspoon vanilla extract

Preheat oven to 450 degrees. Grease an 8-inch square pan.

Sprinkle berries with half of the sugar. Mash berries gently with a spoon. In a medium bowl, sift together flour, remaining sugar, baking powder, and salt. Stir in butter and milk, and mix. The mixture should be lumpy. Spoon the batter into the pan and spread as evenly as possible with a spoon. Bake for 12 to 15 minutes or until a toothpick comes out clean. Let cool and cut into six squares.

Whip cream with powdered sugar and vanilla extract until stiff. Cut shortcake squares horizontally, and spoon berries on the bottom piece and cover with the top piece. Put another spoonful of berries on top, and finish with a dollop of whipped cream. Serve immediately.

Makes 6 servings.

Dinner Plum Cake

1 egg
¼ cup sugar, more or less to taste
2 tablespoons yogurt
1 ½ cups whole wheat pastry flour
1 teaspoon baking soda
¼ teaspoon salt
6 tablespoons melted butter
2 pounds plums
1 ½ tablespoons spreadable fruit of your choice

Preheat oven to 375 degrees, and grease an 11 x 7-inch long pan or a 10-inch round baking pan.

In a medium bowl, beat egg, then add sugar and yogurt, and mix well. Stir together flour, baking soda, and salt. Add to egg mixture. Stir in butter, and press dough into prepared pan, covering bottom and sides. Cut plums into slices and press into dough. Drizzle spreadable fruit over plums.

Bake for 30 to 40 minutes.

Makes 8 servings.

Applesauce Loaf

1 ½ cups applesauce
2 eggs
2 cups whole wheat flour
⅓ cup sugar
¼ cup milk
¼ cup vegetable oil
1 teaspoon baking soda
1 teaspoon ground cinnamon
½ teaspoon baking powder
½ teaspoon ground nutmeg

Preheat oven to 375 degrees, and grease a 9 x 5-inch loaf pan.

Sift together flour, cinnamon, nutmeg, baking soda, and baking powder. In a large bowl, mix together applesauce, oil, milk, eggs, and sugar. Combine dry and wet ingredients, and stir well. Pour mixture into the loaf pan.

Bake for 1 hour or until done. Remove from the pan, and let cool on a wire rack.

Fruit Loaves

1 ½ cups mixed dried fruit (apricots, prunes, or peaches), diced
1 ½ cups dried pears, diced
1 ½ cups dried figs, diced
¼ cup raisins
¼ cup dates, diced
¾ cup apple cider
¼ cup sugar or honey
2 teaspoons grated lemon zest
2 tablespoons lemon juice
3 ½ to 4 cups whole wheat flour
1 ¼ teaspoons salt
1 tablespoon yeast
1 cup milk
2 eggs
1 ½ cups coarsely chopped walnuts or pecans
1 tablespoon ground cinnamon
1 teaspoon aniseed (optional)

At least 10 hours before making the dough, dice the mixed fruit, pears, figs, and raisins, and place in a medium bowl. Heat the cider and sugar in a small saucepan until bubbles appear around the edge. Pour over the fruit. Add the lemon zest and juice. Toss to mix until the fruit is coated. Cover and let steep, stir once or twice. The fruit will absorb most of the liquid.

When you are ready to make the dough, take a large bowl, and mix the yeast and salt with 1 cup flour. Heat the milk to about 120 degrees and gradually add to the dry ingredients. Beat for 2 minutes with an electric mixer at medium speed. Add one egg, ½ cup flour, cinnamon, and ground aniseed. Beat for 2 minutes. Stir in enough of the remaining flour to make a soft dough. Knead on a floured surface until smooth and elastic, about 8 to 10 minutes, using only enough flour to keep the dough from sticking. Place in an oiled bowl, and cover with wax paper and a towel. Let rise in a warm place until double in size, about 1 hour.

Once the dough is done rising, punch it down. On a floured surface, gradually knead in the diced dates, fruit mixture, and nuts, using only enough flour to keep the dough from sticking. Divide in half and shape each half into a 12-inch loaf. Place on a lightly oiled baking sheet. Cover with a towel, and let rise again for 1 to 1 ½ hours.

Beat the remaining egg. Brush the loaves with egg, and bake in a 350-degree oven for 35 to 40 minutes or until golden brown. Cool completely on wire racks.

Cakes 15

Bars & Cookies

Chocolate Chip Pear Bars

½ cup canned pears, drained and diced
5 tablespoons softened butter
⅔ cup milk
1 large egg
2 teaspoons vanilla extract
1 cup quick cooking rolled oats
1 cup unbleached all-purpose flour
½ teaspoon baking soda
¼ teaspoon salt
⅔ cup chocolate chips

Preheat oven to 350 degrees. Lightly spray, oil, or butter a 9-inch square baking pan.

In a large bowl, using an electric mixer or a whisk, cream together the butter and sugar. Then beat in the egg, vanilla extract, and pears. In a medium bowl, whisk together oats, flour, baking soda, and salt. Add the dry ingredients to the wet, and mix. Stir in chocolate chips.

Spread batter into prepared pan. Bake for 25 to 30 minutes or until golden brown on top. Cool in the pan on a rack. Cut into 16 squares.

Lemon Lime Bars

Crust
½ cup butter or margarine
1 cup unbleached all-purpose flour
¼ cup powdered sugar

Filling
1 cup sugar
2 eggs
4 tablespoons lemon juice
½ teaspoon lemon extract
Zest of 1 lime
2 tablespoons of unbleached all-purpose flour
2 teaspoons baking powder

To make the crust, mix butter, flour, and powdered sugar until light and fluffy. Pat into an 8-inch square pan. Bake in a 350-degree oven for 15 minutes.

For the filling, combine sugar, eggs, lemon juice, lemon extract, lime rind, flour, and baking powder. Mix well.

Pour filling over baked crust and bake for 25 to 30 minutes in a 350-degree oven. Remove from the oven, sprinkle with powdered sugar, and cut into bars.

Coconut Macaroon Cookies

1 cup unsweetened shredded coconut

½ cup graham cracker crumbs

½ cup chopped walnuts

¼ teaspoon salt

1 teaspoon baking powder

1 pinch cream of tartar

4 egg whites at room temperature

¾ cup sugar

1 teaspoon vanilla extract

Lightly oil and flour a baking sheet. Preheat oven to 350 degrees.

In a medium bowl, combine coconut, graham cracker crumbs, walnuts, salt, and baking powder. In another bowl, add the cream of tartar to the egg whites, and beat them until they are stiff. Beat in the sugar, 1 tablespoon at a time. Then beat in the vanilla extract. Fold the coconut mixture into the egg whites.

Place tablespoon-size dollops of the mixture on the baking sheet. Bake the cookies for 15 minutes until they are lightly browned and dry. Place on a rack to cool

Makes 40 cookies.

Harvest Cookies

1 ¾ cups unbleached all-purpose flour

½ teaspoon cream of tartar

¾ teaspoon baking soda

¼ teaspoon salt

1 stick unsalted butter at room temperature

¾ cup sugar

1 egg

½ teaspoon lemon extract

¼ teaspoon orange extract

½ teaspoon grated lemon zest

¼ cup dried sweetened cranberries

¼ cup golden raisins

¼ cup dried apricots, finely diced

¼ cup dried blueberries

In a medium bowl, sift together flour, cream of tartar, baking soda, and salt, then lightly whisk and set aside. With an electric mixer on low speed, beat butter until creamy. Switch to medium speed, and add sugar; beat until light and fluffy. Beat in the egg and lemon and orange extracts. Add lemon zest. Blend well, scraping the sides and bottom of bowl as necessary. Turn off the mixer. Add half of the flour mixture, and beat on low speed until blended. The dough will be stiff. Stir in the cranberries, raisins, apricots, and blueberries. Chill the dough for 1 hour.

Once chilled and ready for baking, Preheat oven to 350 degrees. Lightly grease baking sheet and set aside. Take a tablespoon of the dough at a time and roll into a ball. Place on baking sheet. Lightly dip back of fork into flour and flatten the cookies. Bake for 12 to 16 minutes or until golden. Transfer to cooling rack.

Pies

Fruit Custard Pie

1 9-inch pie crust
1 cup sour cream
1 egg
1 teaspoon vanilla extract
¼ teaspoon ground nutmeg
1 tablespoon unbleached all-purpose flour
⅛ teaspoon salt
⅓ cup sugar
2 cups diced fruit (a combination of apples, pears, peaches, or fruit of your choice)

Crumb Topping
⅓ cup unbleached all-purpose flour
1 tablespoon butter
1 tablespoon sugar
1 teaspoon ground cinnamon

Mix together sour cream, egg, vanilla extract, and nutmeg. Add flour, salt, and sugar. Beat until it is a smooth, thin batter. Arrange the diced fruit in the bottom of the pie crust. Then pour the batter over the fruit.

Bake in preheated 400-degree oven for 15 minutes; then reduce the heat to 350 degrees, and bake for 30 more minutes. Remove from the oven and garnish with crumb topping. Increase the oven temperature to 400 degrees, and return the pie to brown for 10 to 15 minutes.

Pineapple Meringue Pie

1 9-inch baked pie crust
2 cups crushed pineapple, drained
1 tablespoon cornstarch
⅓ cup sugar, a little more or less according to taste
1 teaspoon lemon juice
1 tablespoon butter
2 lightly beaten egg yolks
3 egg whites
⅛ teaspoon salt
¼ cup sugar

Preheat oven to 325 degrees.

Combine pineapple, cornstarch, sugar, lemon juice, and butter in saucepan. Cook, stirring until thickened. Pour a little of the pineapple mixture over the egg yolks; mix well. Add the egg mixture to the saucepan. Cook over low heat, stirring constantly until the yolks have thickened. Cool.

Pour the custard into a baked pie crust. Beat egg whites and salt until frothy. Gradually add sugar, continuing to beat until meringue is stiff, smooth, and shiny.

Spread meringue over pie, and bake for 15 minutes or until lightly brown.

Creamy Raspberry Pie

- 1 9-inch baked pie crust
- 2 cups milk
- 1 teaspoon vanilla extract
- 1/2 cup sugar
- 1/3 cup unbleached all-purpose flour
- 1/4 teaspoon salt
- 1 egg
- 4 egg yolks
- 1/4 cup heavy cream, whipped
- 2 10-ounce packages frozen raspberries, drained
- 1/2 cup prepared raspberries or currant glaze

In a double boiler, scald milk. Add vanilla extract and sugar. Combine flour and salt. Slowly pour hot milk into flour until well mixed. Return the mixture to the double boiler, and cook until thick. Beat egg and egg yolks together. Slowly add about 1 cup of the milk mixture to the eggs. Add the egg mixture to the rest of the milk mixture in the double boiler, and continue to cook, stirring constantly until thick. Cool. Fold whipped cream into cool egg mixture. Pour into baked pie crust. Cover with raspberries. Spoon glaze over berries. Chill.

Mixed Fruit Pie

- 1 9-inch pie crust, top and bottom
- 3 tablespoons tapioca
- 1/2 cup apple juice concentrate
- 1 tablespoon fresh lime juice
- 3 medium firm pears, peeled and sliced
- 1/2 pint blackberries
- 1/2 pint blueberries
- 1 tablespoon sugar, optional

In a medium bowl, stir together tapioca, apple juice concentrate, and lime juice. Add sugar to juice mixture, and stir. Add pears and berries, and toss gently. Turn fruit mixture into prepared crust. Cover with top crust, and bake at 400 degrees for 35 minutes or until golden brown.

Makes 8 servings.

Double Blackberry Pie

1 9-inch baked pie crust
2/3 cup sugar
3 tablespoons cornstarch
1/2 teaspoon grated lemon zest
1/4 teaspoon ground cinnamon
3 cups frozen blackberries
1 tablespoon lime juice
3 1/2 cups fresh blackberries

In a small bowl, combine sugar, cornstarch, lemon zest, and cinnamon. In a medium saucepan, combine frozen berries and 1/4 cup water. Bring to a boil over medium heat. Stir in sugar mixture and lime juice. Return to a boil and cook, stirring frequently, until thickened, about 5 minutes. Remove from heat and set aside to cool. Stir 2 cups of the fresh blackberries into the cooked blackberries, and spoon into the pie shell. Top the pie with the remaining 1/2 cup fresh blackberries. Cut and serve.

Blueberries can also be used in this recipe.

Awesome Banana Cream Pie

1 9-inch baked pie crust
3 tablespoons cornstarch
1/4 teaspoon salt
1 2/3 cups water
1 14-ounce can sweetened condensed milk
2 large egg yolks, beaten
2 tablespoons butter or margarine
1 teaspoon vanilla extract
3 or 4 bananas
Lemon juice
Whipped cream

In a medium saucepan, dissolve cornstarch and salt in the water. Stir in condensed milk and egg yolks. Cook and stir on medium heat until thick and bubbly. Remove from the stove. Add butter and vanilla extract. Cool slightly. Slice 2 or 3 bananas. Pour lemon juice over bananas. Drain. Arrange bananas on bottom of prepared pie crust. Pour filling over bananas. Cover and chill for at least 4 hours. When ready to serve, spread whipped cream on top. Use remaining bananas as garnish.

Creamy Blackberry Pie

1 9-inch baked pie crust
1 package berry-flavored gelatin
1 cup boiling water
1 pint vanilla ice cream, softened
1 ¾ cup fresh or frozen blackberries, partially thawed

In a large bowl, combine gelatin and water. Stir until dissolved. Cut ice cream into small chunks, and add to gelatin mixture, one spoonful at a time. Blend with a wire whisk after each addition. Dry berries between paper towels, and fold into gelatin mixture. Spoon into prepared pie crust. Refrigerate or freeze several hours before serving.

Mince Fruit Pie

1 9-inch pie crust
1 lemon
½ orange
½ cup crushed pineapple, reserve ½ cup of the juice
1 large yellow apple, peeled, cored, and diced
1 firm pear, peeled, cored, and diced
⅔ cup dried cranberries, chopped
½ cup dried blueberries, chopped
½ cup sugar
¼ teaspoon salt
¼ teaspoon ground cinnamon
¼ teaspoon cloves
¼ teaspoon ground nutmeg
1 teaspoon vanilla extract

Peel and chop the orange and lemon. Coarsely chop a quarter of each rind. Discard the remaining rind and seeds. Process chopped fruit and rind with pineapple juice in a food processor until blended. Transfer to a large saucepan and add remaining ingredients, except vanilla extract. Cover, and cook over low heat for 15 minutes. Raise heat to medium, and continue cooking for 10 minutes, stirring occasionally. Remove from heat, stir in vanilla extract, and set aside to cool. Spoon cooled mixture into pie crust.

Bake in a preheated 350-degree oven for 45 minutes. Serve warm.

Apple Pie Supreme

1 10-inch pie crust
3 cups sliced cooking apples
1 teaspoon grated lime zest
1 tablespoon fresh lime juice
1 1/2 cups sugar
1/4 cup dried cherries, diced
1/4 cup dried blueberries
1 tablespoon unbleached all-purpose flour

Streusel Topping
1/2 cup unbleached all-purpose flour
1/4 cup sugar or brown sugar
1/4 cup butter
1/2 cup rolled oats
1/2 cup coarsely chopped pecans or walnuts

Preheat oven to 400 degrees.

In a large bowl, mix together apples, lime zest, lime juice, sugar, cherries, blueberries, and flour. Spoon the mixture into the pie crust, and set aside. In a small bowl, combine flour and sugar for the topping. Work butter into the flour mixture with a pastry cutter or with your fingers until the mixture resembles crumbles. Add oats and nuts, and mix well. Spread the topping evenly over the apples.

Bake for 55 to 60 minutes or until the apples are tender and the crust is golden brown. Allow to cool for about 12 minutes before slicing.

Apple Blackberry Cobbler

2 12-ounce bags frozen blackberries
2 Golden Delicious apples, chopped
3/4 cup high fiber bran cereal
1/3 cup sugar
2 tablespoons instant tapioca
1/3 cup blackberry fruit spread
1 cup biscuit mix
1/2 cup milk
1 tablespoon sugar
1 egg

Preheat oven to 350 degrees.

Toss blackberries, apples, cereal, and tapioca together. Place in a shallow 1 1/2-quart baking dish. Dot with 1/3 cup blackberry fruit spread. Combine biscuit mix, milk, sugar, and egg; spoon over fruit.

Bake for 50 minutes or until crust is cooked through. Serve warm or cold with frozen yogurt if desired.

Makes 8 servings.

Puddings & Mousses

Coconut Pudding with Pineapple

3 tablespoons sugar
3 tablespoons cornstarch
2 cups coconut milk, divided
¼ teaspoon salt
1 can crushed pineapple

Combine sugar and cornstarch in a small bowl. Blend in ½ cup coconut milk and salt. Heat remaining 1 ½ cups coconut milk in medium saucepan. Do not boil. Add cornstarch mixture. Cook and stir until thickened. Pour into an 8-inch square dish. Refrigerate until firm. Cut into squares. Serve cold with crushed pineapple.

This is a great tropical treat.

Butterscotch Banana Pudding

2 ½ cups milk
¼ cup cornstarch
¼ cup instant tapioca
2 bananas, peeled and sliced
1 tablespoon vanilla extract
1 cup butterscotch chips
3 tablespoons brown sugar

Mix 1 cup milk with cornstarch and tapioca, and set aside. Place banana slices in a 1 ½-quart dish. Set aside. Heat remaining 1 ½ cups milk over medium heat, and stir in cornstarch-tapioca mixture, vanilla extract, butterscotch chips, and brown sugar. Continue stirring until mixture thickens, about 4 minutes. Remove from heat, and pour over bananas. Refrigerate until ready to serve. Serve warm or cold.

Lime Mousse with Blackberries

¾ cup plus 3 tablespoons sugar
3 tablespoons cornstarch
1 large egg, lightly beaten
1 tablespoon grated lime zest
½ cup fresh lime juice
⅛ teaspoon salt
½ teaspoon unflavored gelatin
⅓ cup heavy cream
3 tablespoons sour cream
1 cup blackberries

In a medium saucepan, combine ¾ cup sugar and cornstarch. Whisk in 1 cup cold water, stirring until smooth. Stir in the egg, and cook over medium heat, whisking constantly until the mixture comes to a boil, about 4 minutes. Remove from heat, and stir in the lime zest, lime juice, and salt. Set aside to cool.

Place ¼ cup cold water in a small bowl and add the gelatin. Let stand for about 4 minutes until softened. Set the bowl over a small saucepan of simmering water and stir until the gelatin dissolves. Set aside to cool. In a medium bowl, with electric mixer, beat the cream and the sour cream until foamy. Beat in the dissolved gelatin mixture.

Fold the cream mixture into the cooled lime mixture. Spoon into dessert glasses, and chill until set, about 2 hours. Top with blackberries, and serve.

Makes 4 servings.

Banana Mousse

4 mashed ripe bananas
3 tablespoons lemon-lime juice
¼ cup sugar
1 teaspoon vanilla extract
1 ½ cups heavy cream
2 tablespoons cookie crumbs, optional

Sprinkle juice on mashed bananas; add sugar and vanilla extract. Mix well. Whip cream, and gently stir the banana mixture into the whipped cream. Pour into dessert glasses. Refrigerate at least 4 hours. When ready to serve, top with cookie crumbs, if desired.

Apricot Whip

1 ½ cups dried apricots
1 cup water
½ cup sugar
1 thin slice lemon with rind
1 cup heavy cream, whipped

In a small saucepan, combine apricots, water, sugar, and lemon. Bring to a boil, cover, and simmer for 20 minutes or until apricots are tender. Cool. Place apricot mixture in blender and process until completely pureed. Whip cream, and fold the apricot puree into the whipped cream. Spoon into individual dessert dishes. Chill for several hours before serving.

Makes 6 servings.

Purple Cow Fondue

1 ½ cups grape juice
2 tablespoons lemon juice
1 pound shredded cheddar cheese
2 tablespoons unbleached all-purpose flour
Pinch of ground nutmeg

Combine grape juice and lemon juice in a fondue pot. Heat on top of the stove until just bubbly. Toss cheese with flour and slowly add to the juice, stirring constantly to prevent lumps. Keep the heat low. When cheese is smooth and sauce-like, transfer it to a fondue pot or other warmer. Sprinkle with nutmeg. Cut and dip apples, pears, or other fruit in the fondue.

Makes 4 servings

Orange Whip

1 ¼ teaspoons grated orange zest
1 ¼ cups orange juice
¾ cup plus 3 tablespoons sugar
⅛ teaspoon salt
3 tablespoons cornstarch
1 egg
1 tablespoon lemon juice
1 teaspoon unflavored gelatin
¼ cup heavy cream
¼ cup sour cream
¼ cup can mandarin oranges, drained

In a medium saucepan, combine orange zest, ½ cup orange juice, and salt. Bring to a boil over medium heat. In a small bowl, combine ¼ cup sugar, cornstarch, and ¼ cup orange juice. Whisk the cornstarch mixture into the orange mixture and cook, whisking, until the mixture comes back to a boil and thickens, about 3 minutes. In a small bowl, lightly beat the egg. Gradually whisk some of the hot orange mixture into the egg, then whisk the warmed egg mixture back into the saucepan and cook, whisking until the mixture just comes to a boil, about 2 minutes. Remove from heat and scrap into a medium bowl. Stir in the lemon juice and the remaining ½ cup orange juice. Let cool to room temperature.

Place ¼ cup cold water in a small bowl, add the gelatin, and let stand until softened, about 4 minutes. Set the bowl over a small saucepan of simmering water, and stir until the gelatin dissolves, about 3 minutes. Cool the mixture.

In a large bowl, with an electric mixer, beat the cream and sour cream until foamy. Gradually stir in the remaining 3 tablespoons sugar, beating until soft peaks form. Mix in the dissolved gelatin until well combined. Fold the cream mixture into the orange mixture, and spoon into bowls. Chill until set, about 2 hours. Garnish with mandarin oranges.

Baked Pears & Raspberry Fondue

⅓ cup butter
¼ cup honey
3 egg yolks
1 cup cookie crumbs
½ cup raspberries
½ cup finely chopped pears
3 egg whites
¼ teaspoon salt
¼ teaspoon almond extract

Preheat oven to 325 degrees, and butter a 1-quart casserole dish.

Cream butter until soft. Add honey slowly, and beat until light and fluffy. Add egg yolks, one at a time, beating well after each addition. Add cookie crumbs, raspberries, and pears to the mixture. Beat egg whites until foamy, then add salt, and beat until stiff. Do not over beat. Fold the egg whites into the yolk and fruit mixture, then add the almond extract. Pour into the casserole dish, and bake for 30 minutes or until lightly brown. Serve immediately.

Makes 4 to 5 servings.

Soups & Compotes

Festive Apple & Pear Compote

2 Red or Golden Delicious apples, cored and thinly sliced
2 fresh pears, cored and thinly sliced
1 cup grapes, halved and seeded
1 cup cranberry juice cocktail
1 cup ginger ale
Flaked coconut

Toss fruits together. Combine cranberry juice and ginger ale, and pour over fruit mixture. Chill thoroughly. Sprinkle with coconut before serving.

Wintertime Compote

1 cup dried apricots
1 cup dried cherries
½ cup raisins
½ teaspoon grated fresh ginger
1 teaspoon grated orange zest
1 ⅔ cups orange juice
¼ cup sugar

In a small saucepan, combine apricots, cherries, raisins, ginger, orange zest, orange juice, and sugar. Gently simmer for about 15 minutes. Remove from heat, and set aside for the flavors to blend.

Chilled Fruit Stew

3 cups cubed cantaloupe or honeydew
½ cup orange or pineapple juice
½ cup vanilla yogurt
2 tablespoons sugar or honey
1 teaspoon finely chopped fresh ginger
2 teaspoons lime juice
2 cups chopped peaches
1 cup blueberries

Process first six ingredients in food processor until smooth. Toss peaches and blueberries together and place into bowl and chill. Pour chilled cantaloupe melon mixture over peaches and blueberries. Stir to mix. Serve in individual dessert bowls.

Zesty Peach Soup

1 ½ peaches, peeled, pitted, and cut into small pieces
1 ½ cups cubed cantaloupe
1 ¼ cups peach nectar
½ cup cranberry juice
Juice of 1 lime
1 tablespoon sugar
Raspberries and mint leaves for garnishing

Place cantaloupe, peaches, peach nectar, cranberry juice, and lime juice in blender, and process until smooth. Pour into a container and refrigerate until chilled. Pour soup into serving bowls. Garnish with berries and mint leaves.

Three Berry Soup

3 cups white grape juice
$1/4$ cup purple grape juice
2 cups mixed berries
$1/3$ cup sugar
1 tablespoon cornstarch
$1/4$ teaspoon ground cinnamon
Sour cream or yogurt

Heat the white grape juice in a saucepan over medium heat. Stir in berries and sugar, and reduce heat to medium low and cook for 5 minutes. Combine cornstarch with purple grape juice. Stir cornstarch mixture and cinnamon into soup, and cook for 2 more minutes. Remove from heat and cool. Refrigerate until chilled. Pour soup into serving bowls. Serve with dollops of sour cream or yogurt.

Baked & Broiled Fruit Dishes

Honey Baked Goldies

3 Golden Delicious apples, cored
½ cup honey
¼ cup golden raisins
½ cup chopped walnuts
¼ cup lime juice
¼ cup water
½ teaspoon ground cinnamon
1 teaspoon ground nutmeg
Vanilla ice cream or half and half

Remove a third of the peel from the top of the apples. Place in an 8-inch baking dish. Combine remaining ingredients in saucepan, except ice cream, and bring to a boil. Pour the boiling mixture over and around apples. Bake uncovered in a 350-degree oven for 1 hour or until apples are tender. Baste every 15 minutes. Serve warm with half and half or cold with ice cream

Baked Pears

6 firm pears, cored and sliced
⅓ cup honey
1 teaspoon vanilla extract
½ cup slivered almonds
2 tablespoons butter
1 cup yogurt

Preheat oven to 350 degrees and grease a 9-inch baking dish.

Core and slice pears (peel only if skin is tough), and arrange in rows in prepared dish. Mix honey and vanilla extract, and drizzle over pears. Top with almonds and dot with butter.

Bake in preheated oven for 10 to 15 minutes or until pears are tender. Baste frequently during baking with pear juice. Serve hot or cold, topped with yogurt

Makes 6 servings.

Sunny Poached Pears

3 firm pears, peeled and cubed
1 cup pineapple juice
2/3 cup peach spreadable fruit
2 teaspoons grated orange zest
2 tablespoons orange juice

Mix all ingredients in 10-inch skillet. Heat to boiling; reduce heat to low and simmer uncovered for 25 minutes or until pears are tender. Spoon juice over pears occasionally.

Oven Baked Fruits

1 orange
1 lemon
3 tablespoons light brown sugar
1 28-ounce can apricots, drained
1 8-ounce can pineapple chunks, drained
1 8-ounce can sliced peaches, drained
1 8-ounce can pitted cherries, drained
Nutmeg
1 8-ounce carton sour cream

Grate orange and lemon rinds into brown sugar. Cut orange and lemon into thin slices. Mix with other fruit. Layer in a 1 1/2-quart casserole dish and sprinkle with sugar and dashes of nutmeg. Bake in a preheated 300-degree oven for 30 minutes. Serve hot, topped with sour cream

This is a really good way to get your servings of fruit.

Baked & Broiled Fruit Dishes

Broiled Pineapples & Plums

1 whole fresh pineapple
3 red plums, sliced
2 tablespoons honey
4 tablespoons butter

Slice pineapple, skin and all, into ½-inch slices. Peel the slices, and cut out the eyes. Place pineapple and plum slices on buttered baking sheet. Drizzle honey over the slices, and dot with butter. Broil about 5 to 7 minutes or until slightly browned.

Makes 4 servings.

Microwaved Baked Apples

2 cooking apples
⅓ cup apple juice
2 slices fresh ginger
1 cinnamon stick
3 orange slices
½ cup low fat yogurt
1 tablespoon maple syrup

Peel the top third of each apple. Place in a microwaveable dish. Add apple juice, ginger, cinnamon, and orange slices. Cover with plastic wrap and microwave for 5 minutes. Let stand for 5 minutes. Halve or quarter the apples. Place 1 tablespoon of the cooking liquid in a cup, and add yogurt and maple syrup to the liquid. Drizzle over the apples. Garnish as desired.

Peach Royale

8 large fresh or frozen peach halves

1 peach half, mashed

$1/2$ cup cookie crumbs

1 tablespoon sugar

1 tablespoon soft butter

1 large egg yolk

2 tablespoons slivered almonds

2 tablespoons lime juice

Preheat oven to 375 degrees, and grease a shallow baking dish large enough to accommodate peach halves.

Place the peach halves in the prepared baking dish. Mix the mashed peach half, cookie crumbs, sugar, butter, and egg yolk. Fill peach halves with mixture and dot with almonds. Sprinkle lime juice over tops, and bake in preheated oven for 25 minutes.

Apple Fritters

2 egg yolks

$1/2$ cup sugar

1 cup yogurt

2 cups whole wheat pastry flour

$1/2$ teaspoon ground nutmeg

$1/2$ teaspoon salt

$1/2$ teaspoon baking soda

1 tablespoon melted butter

2 egg whites, beaten stiff

4 firm apples, cored and cut into $1/4$-inch thick chunks

$1/2$ cup oil

Beat egg yolks with sugar until smooth and light. Add yogurt, and stir until smooth. Stir together flour, nutmeg, salt, and baking soda. Add to egg mixture. Stir in melted butter; then fold in egg whites.

In a heavy iron skillet, put enough oil to measure about $1/4$ inch deep. Heat oil to 370 degrees. Dip apple chunks into batter, then fry in hot oil until golden brown on both sides. Keep fritters warm until all apples and batter has been used.

Apple Harvest Casserole

4 apples, unpeeled and cubed
2 oranges, peeled and chopped
1 cup raisins
1 cup chopped nuts
2/3 cup maple syrup
1/4 teaspoon salt
1/2 teaspoon ground cinnamon
1/2 teaspoon ground nutmeg

Mix all ingredients together, and spoon into a medium-sized casserole dish. Bake in a 400-degree oven for about 45 minutes or until apples are tender.

Breakfast Fruit Treats

Breakfast Fruit Salad

1 grapefruit, peeled and sectioned
1 orange, peeled and sectioned
1 apple, chopped
1 banana, sliced
½ cup blueberries
1 cup orange or pineapple juice
1 cup cottage cheese
½ cup chopped almonds

Cut the orange and grapefruit sections in half. Combine all the fruit in a bowl. Mix in the fruit juice, and spoon into dessert glasses. Top with the cottage cheese and almonds.

Makes 4 servings.

Breakfast Banana Split

2 tablespoons peanut butter
2 tablespoons fruit juice
1 banana
3 tablespoons granola or chopped nuts
½ cup cottage cheese

Blend the peanut butter and fruit juice together. Spread the mixture on the banana. Then roll the banana in the granola. Slice the banana, and place into a bowl. Top with cottage cheese.

Hot Apple Granola

½ cup granola
⅔ cup apple juice
1 chopped apple
2 tablespoons raisins
¼ teaspoon ground cinnamon

Combine the granola, apple juice, chopped apple, raisins, and cinnamon in a 1-quart saucepan. Bring to a boil over low heat, and simmer for 1 minute, stirring often. Serve warm.

Sundae Fruit Breakfast Delight

4 frozen waffles
2 sliced bananas
2 8-ounce containers fruit flavored yogurt
1 cup fresh strawberries, sliced
1 cup fresh blueberries
½ cup whole-grain cereal
Strawberry syrup

Toast waffles according to package directions. Cut into quarters. Place banana slices evenly in serving bowls. Layer with half each of yogurt, berries, and cereal. Repeat layer once. Top each with the waffle quarters. Serve with syrup.

Blueberry Applesauce Muffins

1 cup oat bran

⅓ cup whole wheat flour

½ cup bran

2 teaspoons baking powder

⅓ teaspoon ground cinnamon

2 tablespoons brown sugar

¼ teaspoon salt

2 egg whites

⅓ cup applesauce

1 cup milk

½ cup blueberries

In a large bowl, combine oat bran, wheat flour, bran, baking powder, cinnamon, brown sugar, and salt. Set aside. In a small bowl, combine egg whites and applesauce. Whisk in milk. Pour liquid into flour mixture in the large bowl. Mix until moistened, and then fold in blueberries. Spoon batter into 12 muffin cups coated with nonstick spray.

Bake in a 425-degree oven for 15 to 18 minutes or until muffins are lightly brown.

Smoothies, Sorbets, & Drinks

Grape Ice

1 cup unsweetened red grape juice
1 tablespoon chopped lemon with peel
2 teaspoons sugar
1 cup ice cubes

Put juice, lemon, and sugar in blender. Blend on medium speed until lemon is pureed. Add ice cubes and process at high speed until mixture is a snowy consistency.

Watermelon Slush

6 cups watermelon, peeled, seeded, and cubed
1/3 cup sugar
2 1/2 tablespoons lemon juice

Blend watermelon in food processor until smooth. Pour into a bowl. Add sugar and lemon juice, stirring until sugar dissolves. Cover and chill. Pour mixture into a 9 x 13-inch pan and freeze, stirring occasionally. Leave in freezer for about 3 hours or until firm. Scoop frozen mixture into balls when ready to serve.

This is a great way to use leftover watermelon.

Apricot Bliss

1 15-ounce can apricot halves, drained
¼ cup juice from can
¼ cup apricot preserves
1 cup crushed ice

Place all ingredients in blender, and blend until smooth.

Peach Refresher

1 cup ice
½ cup plain or nonfat yogurt
1 cup frozen sliced peaches
½ cup frozen raspberries
½ cup orange juice

Crush ice in blender. Add remaining ingredients; blend until smooth.

Raspberry Cocoa Chiller

1 cup frozen raspberries
1 cup vanilla ice cream
²/₃ cup milk
1 tablespoon cocoa powder

Place berries and milk in blender, and blend until smooth. Add cocoa and ice cream, and blend again.

Berry Smoothie

1 large banana
1 8-ounce can pineapple chunks, undrained
1 cup frozen mixed berries, partially thawed
1 8-ounce carton blueberry yogurt

Slice banana, and place in blender. Add pineapple chunks with juice, mixed berries, and yogurt. Cover, and blend until smooth.

Kiwi Cooler

5 kiwi fruit
½ cup sugar
2 teaspoons cornstarch
1 cup frozen whipped topping, thawed
2 drops green food coloring, optional

Peel kiwi, cut into chunks, and puree in food processor. In a small saucepan, whisk together ½ cup puree, sugar, cornstarch, and water. Simmer over medium heat, stirring constantly, until mixture thickens, about 4 to 5 minutes. Remove from heat, and transfer mixture to a medium bowl. Let cool, then stir in remaining kiwi puree and refrigerate until chilled. Gently fold in whipped topping and food coloring, if desired. Spoon into individual serving dishes, and chill until set, about 3 hours. Garnish with sliced kiwi, if desired.

Purple Sherbet

¾ cup sugar
2 tablespoons maple syrup
1 teaspoon grated lime zest
½ teaspoon ground ginger
⅛ teaspoon ground allspice
⅛ teaspoon salt
4 cups frozen blueberries
2 tablespoons cornstarch
2 ½ cups buttermilk
1 tablespoon fresh lime juice

In a medium saucepan, combine ½ cup sugar, maple syrup, lime zest, ginger, allspice, and salt. Stir in blueberries, and cook over medium heat, stirring frequently, until the berries are tender and syrupy, about 7 minutes. In a small bowl, combine the remaining ¼ cup sugar and cornstarch. Stir the cornstarch mixture into the simmering blueberries, and cook, stirring constantly, until thickened, about 2 minutes. Remove from heat and cool to room temperature. Stir in the buttermilk and lime juice. Transfer to an ice cream maker and process according to manufacturer's directions.

Orange Banana Slush

½ cup egg substitute
½ cup frozen orange juice concentrate
1 banana
1 cup milk
1 tablespoon sugar
6 slightly crushed ice cubes

Combine all ingredients in a blender. Process until slushy.

Mango & Blueberry Smoothie

1 ¼ cups milk
1 ½ cups chilled orange juice
1 mango, peeled, seeded, and cut
   into chunks
1 cup frozen blueberries

Combine all ingredients in a food processor or blender. Process until smooth.

Blueberry Sorbet

16 ounces frozen blueberries

6 ounces frozen apple juice concentrate

2 tablespoons sugar

1/4 cup water or more

1 teaspoon lemon juice

Combine berries, apple juice, and sugar in a food processor or blender. Add water and lemon juice. Process until smooth. Serve immediately or store in freezer until ready to serve.

Watermelon Sunset

3 slices watermelon, 1-inch thick

1 1/2 cups blackberries

2 medium pears

1/4 cup peach nectar

Cut each watermelon slice into 10 wedges and remove rind and seeds. Arrange wedges on six plates. Top with blackberries. Refrigerate for at least 1 hour. Peel and core pears, and cut into fourths. Place pears and nectar in food processor, and process until smooth. Spoon sauce over watermelon and blackberries and serve.

Makes 6 servings.

Honeydew Sorbet

1 honeydew, peeled and cut into
   1-inch pieces
2 tablespoons sugar
2 tablespoons lemon juice

Place honeydew, sugar, and lemon juice in blender or food processor. Cover and blend until smooth. Pour into 9-inch square pan. Cover and freeze for 1 to 1 $\frac{1}{2}$ hours or until partially frozen. Once the mixture is frozen, spoon it into a blender or food processor. Cover and blend until smooth. Return the mixture to the pan. Cover and freeze for another 2 hours or until firm. Let stand for 10 minutes at room temperature before spooning into dessert dishes. Or pour into ice cream maker and process according to manufacturer's directions.

Makes 6 servings.

Summer Fruit Breeze

1 cup raspberries
1 cup chopped peaches
1 cup pineapple chunks
1 cup sugar, optional
1 cup plain yogurt

Place fruit and sugar, if desired, in food processor. Process until smooth. Freeze for 2 $\frac{1}{2}$ hours or until firm. Place frozen mixture and yogurt in food processor. Cover and blend until smooth. Spoon soft ice into glasses, or refreeze about 1 hour or until firm.

Makes 6 servings.

Pineapple Freezie

4 cups pineapple chunks
½ cup sugar
2 tablespoons lemon juice
1 teaspoon grated orange zest

Place all ingredients in food processor. Process until smooth. Pour into 9 x 5 x 3-inch loaf pan. Cover and freeze about 2 hours or until firm around edges but soft in the center. Spoon partially frozen mixture into food processor. Process until smooth. Return the mixture to the pan. Cover and freeze about 3 hours or until firm. Let stand for 10 minutes at room temperature before spooning into dessert dishes. Or pour into ice cream maker and process according to manufacturer's directions.

Makes 6 servings.

Peachy Mint Sorbet

2 cups peach nectar
¼ cup sugar
1 large ripe peach, cut into pieces
1 tablespoon grated fresh ginger
1 ½ tablespoons minced fresh mint

Heat 1 cup nectar and sugar in small saucepan over medium heat, stirring until sugar dissolves. Remove from heat, and cool. Place remaining nectar and peach pieces in blender, and process until smooth. Combine cooled nectar, peach mixture, ginger, and mint in an ice cream maker, and freeze according to manufacturer's directions. When almost firm, serve, or store in plastic container until ready to serve.

Makes 6 servings.

Summer Citrus Punch

²⁄₃ cup boiling water
4 regular size plain tea bags
¹⁄₂ cup sugar, more or less to taste
2 cups cold water
¹⁄₄ cup lime juice
1 cup orange juice
1 12-ounce can lemon-lime soft drink, chilled

Pour boiling water over tea bags. Cover and steep for 5 minutes. Remove and discard tea bags. Stir in sugar, cold water, lime juice, and orange juice. Chill for 1 hour. Stir in soft drink, and serve.

Enjoy this punch on a hot humid afternoon.

Party Punch

¹⁄₄ cup sugar
1 cup water
1 cup pink grapefruit juice
1 cup white grape juice
1 cup pineapple juice
1 liter chilled ginger ale

Bring sugar and water to a boil in a large saucepan, stirring constantly, until sugar dissolves. Cool, and stir in the other juices. Transfer juice to a punch bowl, and pour in the chilled ginger ale. Serve.

Makes 8 servings.

This is one party punch your guests will love.

Strawberry Milk Punch

1 10-ounce package frozen strawberries in syrup, thawed
1 cup strawberry ice cream
2 cups milk
1 12-ounce can lemon-lime soda

In a blender, place strawberries, ice cream, and milk. Blend on high speed until smooth. Pour mixture into a small punch bowl. Just before serving, pour soda into milk mixture and stir gently. Serve immediately.

Fruit Punch

1 1/2 cups sugar
1 cup water
1/4 cup light corn syrup
1/4 cup grated lemon zest
2/3 cup fresh lemon juice
1 quart pineapple juice
2 cups orange juice
1 liter club soda, chilled

Bring the first three ingredients to a boil in a saucepan, stirring constantly. Stir in lemon zest. Reduce heat, and simmer for 5 minutes. Cool. Stir in lemon juice, pineapple juice, and orange juice. Cover, and chill for 8 hours. Stir in club soda, and serve immediately.

Relishes & Salads

Going Green Salad

2 kiwi fruit, peeled and sliced
1 cup cubed honeydew
²/₃ cup seedless green grapes, halved
1 unpeeled ripe green pear, sliced
²/₃ cup ricotta cheese
¹/₃ cup honey
¹/₂ cup lime juice
1 teaspoon grated lime zest
1 teaspoon vanilla extract

Toss together first four ingredients, and set aside. Combine ricotta cheese and honey, and mix well. Add the other three ingredients, and stir. Serve the cheese mixture with the salad.

Refreshing Kiwi Salad

6 cups spinach leaves
6 kiwi fruits, peeled and sliced
4 11-ounce cans mandarin oranges, drained
1 avocado, peeled, pitted, and diced
1 tablespoon honey
2 teaspoons canola oil
¹/₄ cup orange juice
2 tablespoons lime juice

Layer spinach, kiwi, oranges, and avocado on individual salad plates. In a small bowl, whisk together honey and oil. Slowly whisk in orange juice and lime juice. Drizzle over salad.

Makes 6 servings

Springtime Fruit Salad

2 kiwi fruits, peeled and sliced
²/₃ cup strawberries, sliced
¹/₃ cup blueberries
1 ¹/₂ pears, peeled and thinly sliced
2 sliced plums
¹/₂ cup walnut pieces
Lettuce leaves

Dressing
¹/₄ cup orange juice
2 tablespoons honey
1 tablespoon lime juice

Toss together first six ingredients of the salad, and place on top of lettuce leaves. Blend all of the dressing ingredients together, and drizzle over the salad.

Cranberry Salad

1 15-ounce can whole cranberry sauce
1 8-ounce can crushed pineapple, drained
1 teaspoon lime juice
1 8-ounce carton sour cream
1 tablespoon sugar, optional

Combine all ingredients, and stir until well blended. Pour mixture into an 8 ¹/₂ x 4 ¹/₂-inch loaf pan. Cover and freeze until firm. After removing from the freezer, cut into 1-inch slices, and serve on lettuce leaves, if desired.

Makes 8 servings.

Creamy Ambrosia Mold

1 envelope unflavored gelatin
½ cup water
1 15 ½-ounce can pineapple chunks, undrained
⅓ cup sugar
Juice of 1 lemon
2 3-ounce packages cream cheese, softened
1 ½ cups mandarin oranges
½ cup chopped walnuts
½ cup flaked coconut

Sprinkle gelatin over cold water, and let stand for 1 minute. Drain pineapple. Reserve juice and set pineapple chunks aside. Add enough water to the juice to make 1 cup. Place juice in a 2-quart saucepan, and heat to boiling. Add gelatin mixture, and stir until gelatin dissolves. Remove from heat. Stir in sugar, lemon juice, and cream cheese, using a wire whisk to blend. Chill until the mixture is the consistency of unbeaten egg whites. Fold in pineapple chunks, orange sections, walnuts, and coconut. Spoon mixture into a lightly oiled mold; cover and chill until firm. Flip the mold on a bed of lettuce leaves.

Makes 6 servings.

Pineapple Apricot Salad

2 3-ounce packages apricot-flavored gelatin
½ cup cold water
1 8-ounce can crushed pineapple, undrained
1 ½ cups buttermilk
1 8-ounce container frozen whipped topping, thawed

Soften gelatin in cold water in a small saucepan for 1 minute. Add pineapple, and cook for 5 to 10 minutes until gelatin dissolves, stirring often. Remove from heat, and stir in buttermilk and container of whipped topping. Pour mixture into a lightly oiled 7-cup mold. Cover and chill for 1 hour or until mixture is firm. Garnish if desired.

Fruit Salad with Dried Cherries

1 grapefruit, peeled and sectioned
1 banana, peeled and sliced
1 apple, cored and chopped
1 pear, cored and chopped
3 tablespoons golden raisins
$1/3$ cup dried cherries or blueberries
$1/2$ cup orange juice
1 tablespoon honey
1 teaspoon sunflower seeds, optional

In a medium bowl, combine the fruit. Mix together the juice and honey, and pour over the fruit. Sprinkle with sunflower seeds if desired.

Apple Salad with Dates

2 cups diced apples
$1/2$ cup chopped dates
$1/2$ cup diced celery
$1/4$ cup mayonnaise
2 tablespoons apple juice
Salad greens

Toss together the apples, dates, and celery. Blend together the mayonnaise and apple juice. Pour the mayonnaise mixture over the apple mixture, and stir. Serve on a bed of salad greens.

Cran-Pear Relish

1 15-ounce can whole cranberry sauce
1 cup pears, peeled and diced
²⁄₃ cup mandarin oranges, drained and coarsely chopped
¼ cup chopped walnuts
1 teaspoon grated orange zest

Mix ingredients together, and chill for at least an hour. Serve.

Strawberry Orange Relish

3 to 4 oranges
2 cups fresh strawberries, hulled and sliced
2 tablespoons orange extract
2 tablespoons granulated sugar
½ cup currant jelly
¼ teaspoon fresh lemon juice

Peel the oranges and cut crosswise into 5 or 6 slices. Layer the slices in a shallow serving bowl, drizzle with orange extract, and set aside. In a small bowl, combine the strawberries and sugar; set aside for 30 minutes. In a small saucepan over medium low heat, melt the jelly, and stir in the lemon juice. Pour the warm jelly over the strawberries, and mix well. Spoon the strawberries and sauce over the oranges, and set aside for at least 45 minutes before serving.

Cranberry Pear Medley

1 cup dried cranberries

3 cups pears or apples, peeled and chopped

1 teaspoon grated lemon zest

¼ cup pecan pieces, optional

In a medium bowl, combine the ingredients and mix well. Serve with plain yogurt, if desired

Miscellaneous Desserts & Snacks

Festive Fruit Pizza

Crust

¾ **cup butter or margarine**

⅔ **cup sugar**

3 **cups unbleached all-purpose flour**

¼ **cup milk**

Glaze

¼ **cup sugar**

1 **tablespoon cornstarch**

¾ **cup fresh orange juice**

Cheese Filling

1 **8-ounce package cream cheese, softened**

¼ **cup sugar**

2 **tablespoons sour cream**

½ **teaspoon grated lemon zest**

½ **teaspoon vanilla extract**

Topping

Sliced peaches, strawberries, kiwi fruit, mandarin oranges, blueberries, or your choice of fruit

Preheat oven to 400 degrees.

Beat butter and sugar in a small bowl on medium speed with electric mixer until light and fluffy, about 1 to 2 minutes. Gradually add flour and milk. Mix until thoroughly combined. Press dough onto a 12-inch round pizza pan to form crust. Bake for 13 to 18 minutes or until light and golden brown. Cool on wire rack.

Meanwhile, to prepare glaze, combine sugar and cornstarch in a saucepan. Add juice, and cook over medium heat, stirring constantly, until mixture comes to a boil. Boil for 1 to 2 minutes. Then remove from heat, and cool for 10 minutes.

For the cheese filling, beat cream cheese, sugar, sour cream, and lemon zest in a small bowl with an electric mixer until smooth.

Spoon the cheese filling onto the cooled crust. Arrange fruit on cheese mixture. To finish, drizzle glaze over fruit. Cut into wedges, and serve.

Double Fruit Crisp

1 15-ounce can peaches
1 15-ounce can pears
1 tablespoon cornstarch
1/3 cup unbleached all-purpose flour
1/4 cup light brown sugar
2 tablespoons sugar
1/2 cup finely chopped walnuts
1/2 teaspoon ground cinnamon
1/4 teaspoon ground nutmeg
2 tablespoons cooking oil

Preheat oven to 400 degrees. Lightly spray a 9-inch pie pan.

Drain syrup from fruit in a medium saucepan. Chop fruit into chunks, and place in prepared baking dish. Whisk cornstarch into fruit syrup in saucepan, and cook over medium high heat, stirring frequently, until mixture clears and comes to a boil. Then pour over fruit in the baking dish.

In a medium bowl, whisk together flour, sugar, nuts, and spices. Add cooking oil and stir with a fork until crumbly. Sprinkle nut topping over fruit.

Bake for 25 to 30 minutes or until topping is lightly browned. Serve warm at room temperature.

Dinner Dates

2 cups dates, pitted and chopped
1/2 cup butter or margarine
1/2 cup honey
1 egg
1 teaspoon vanilla extract
2 cups chopped walnuts
1/3 cup flaked coconut

Mix dates, butter, honey, egg, and vanilla extract in a saucepan. Bring to a boil, and boil for 1 minute. Cool. Stir in the nuts. Form into 1-inch balls, and roll in coconut. Store in the refrigerator until ready to serve.

Chocolate Dipped Fruits

3 ounces bittersweet chocolate
12 dried apricots
12 dried peach slices
3 tablespoons chopped pecans or walnuts

Microwave the chocolate on high for 2 minutes, stirring halfway through. Dip the apricots and peaches halfway into the chocolate. Let the excess drip off. Place the fruits onto wax paper. Sprinkle nuts over the chocolate-covered portions, and place them in the refrigerator so that the chocolate sets.

Makes 8 servings.

Better-for-you Banana Split

1 medium banana, sliced lengthwise
3 scoops of your favorite frozen yogurt
1/2 cup spreadable fruit
Orange or apple juice
Chopped nuts
Lite whipped topping
Cherry, optional

Place banana halves in banana split dish. Place the scoops of yogurt on banana halves. Add a little fruit juice to the spreadable fruit, blending well. Drizzle over yogurt. Sprinkle nuts over yogurt, and top with whipped topping. Finish with a cherry, if desired.

This is a nice little change from the traditional banana split.

Banana Bonanza with Strawberries

1 ripe banana
2 cups sliced strawberries
1 tablespoon honey or sugar
½ teaspoon vanilla extract
1 ½ cups milk or yogurt

Combine the banana, strawberries, honey, and vanilla extract in a blender, and process until smooth. Add the milk and blend for another minute. Serve immediately in chilled glasses.

Berries with Warm Vanilla Sauce

½ cup applesauce
⅔ cup egg product
1 egg white
1 teaspoon vanilla extract
¼ teaspoon almond extract
1 ½ tablespoons sugar
4 cups mixed berries

Mix all ingredients except berries in a heavy 2-quart saucepan. Heat over low heat, stirring constantly, until mixture is warm. Beat on medium speed for about 10 minutes or until mixture is double in volume. Serve immediately over berries.

Apple-Blueberry Crumble

2 ½ cups frozen blueberries, thawed
2 ⅔ cups chopped apples
¼ cup golden raisins
1 cup unbleached all-purpose flour
2 tablespoons butter
2 tablespoons sugar
1 tablespoon packed brown sugar
1 teaspoon ground cinnamon

Topping
1 cup applesauce
1 cup vanilla yogurt

Preheat oven to 375 degrees. Spray an 8-inch square pan with nonstick cooking spray.

In a medium bowl, mix blueberries, apples, and raisins. In a small bowl, combine flour, sugar, brown sugar, cinnamon, and butter until crumbly, and sprinkle over the fruit mixture.

Bake for 25 to 30 minutes or until brown. Serve warm or chilled, with or without the topping.

Cran-Blue Brownies

1 cup applesauce
½ cup sugar
1 teaspoon vanilla extract
½ cup whole wheat flour
½ cup unbleached all-purpose flour
⅓ cup cocoa powder
1 ½ tablespoons baking powder
½ teaspoon salt
1 egg
½ cup milk
2 tablespoons canola oil
⅓ cup chopped walnut pieces
½ cup dried chopped cranberries
½ cup fresh or frozen blueberries

Preheat oven to 350 degrees, and spray an 8-inch baking pan with cooking spray.

In a medium bowl, combine applesauce, sugar, and vanilla extract. In another bowl, whisk together flour, cocoa, baking powder, and salt. Make a well in the center, and add wet ingredients. Mix until just combined. Fold in walnuts, cranberries, and blueberries. If mixture is too stiff, add a little more applesauce. Spread into prepared pan, and bake for 25 to 30 minutes or until center is firm and not sticky. Cool before slicing.

Makes 6 servings.

Anytime Banana Muffins

1 ½ cups unbleached all-purpose flour

½ cup wheat germ

½ cup packed brown sugar

2 ½ teaspoons baking powder

1 ½ teaspoons pumpkin pie spice

½ teaspoon salt

¾ cup mashed bananas

¾ cup milk

3 tablespoon butter, melted

2 eggs, lightly beaten

Topping

3 tablespoons wheat germ

2 tablespoons packed brown sugar

1 tablespoon unbleached all-purpose flour

1 tablespoon butter, melted

⅛ teaspoon pumpkin pie spice

Preheat oven to 400 degrees. Spray bottoms of muffin cups with nonstick cooking spray.

In a large bowl, combine flour, wheat germ, brown sugar, baking powder, pumpkin pie spice, and salt; mix well. In a medium bowl, combine banana, milk, butter, and eggs; mix well. Add wet ingredients to dry ingredients, and stir just until dry ingredients are moistened.

In a small bowl, combine dry topping ingredients; stir and add butter. Set aside.

Fill muffin cups almost full. Sprinkle topping evenly over batter, patting gently with the back of a spoon. Bake for 22 minutes or until a toothpick comes out clean. Cool on a wire rack for a few minutes before removing muffins from pan. Serve warm.

Makes 12 muffins.

Coconut Date Balls

2 cups dates, pitted and finely chopped
¼ cup maple syrup
½ cup milk
½ teaspoon vanilla extract
1 cup finely chopped pecans
1 ½ cups grated coconut

In a heavy saucepan, cook dates, syrup, and milk over low heat, stirring constantly until thickened, about 5 minutes. Remove from heat, and add vanilla extract, nuts, and coconut. When mixture has completely cooled, form into 1-inch balls. Place on wax paper. This treat may be stored in the refrigerator or freezer. Serve at room temperature.

Chill Out Berry Consommé

2 10-ounce packages frozen raspberries, thawed
2 cups raspberry/cranberry juice
2 ½ cups water
1 tablespoon lime juice
1 cinnamon stick
⅓ cup sugar
2 tablespoons cornstarch
Whipping cream

Combine first five ingredients in a large saucepan. Bring to a boil; reduce heat, and simmer for 15 minutes. Press raspberry mixture through a mesh strainer into a bowl, discarding the seeds. Return to the saucepan, reserving a ¼ cup raspberry liquid. Combine cornstarch and raspberry liquid, and stir until smooth. Bring liquid mixture to a boil. Reduce heat to low, and stir in cornstarch mixture. Cook, stirring constantly, until slightly thickened. Pour into large bowl. Cover and chill for 8 hours. Ladle into bowls. Serve with whipped cream.

Cherry Sweet Dream

2 cups dried cherries
$1/3$ cup sugar
2 cups Granny Smith apples, unpeeled and diced
1 cup seedless grapes, halved
$1/2$ cup walnut pieces
$1/4$ teaspoon salt
1 cup heavy cream, whipped

Place cherries and sugar in food processor, and process until coarsely chopped. Cover and chill in the refrigerator overnight. Add apples, grapes, walnuts, and salt. Fold in whipped cream. Chill for at least 4 more hours. Garnish as desired.

Spicy Raisins

1 cup golden raisins
1 cup regular raisins
$2/3$ cup canola oil
Salt
Chili powder

Combine raisins and oil in saucepan. Cook for 8 to 10 minutes until raisins are plump. Drain on paper towels. Sprinkle with salt and chili powder.

Summer Soother

1 14-ounce can condensed milk
1 cup pineapple juice
2 medium bananas, sliced
⅓ cup club soda
9 or 10 ice cubes

Process all ingredients in a blender until smooth.

Pineapple & Grapes with Strawberry Sauce

3 cups pineapple tidbits, drained
3 cups seedless grapes
⅔ cup strawberry sauce
Mint leaves

Strawberry Sauce
1 10-ounce package frozen strawberries, partially thawed
¼ cup sugar
1 tablespoon lemon juice

Combine pineapple and grapes, and chill. Place strawberry sauce ingredients in a blender, and process until smooth. When ready to serve, put fruit into individual dessert dishes, cover with strawberry sauce, and garnish with mint leaves.

Little Fruit Gems

2 cups mixed dried fruit pieces, chop pieces if too large
2 cups shredded coconut
½ cup crunchy peanut butter
1 teaspoon vanilla extract

In a large bowl, mix together all ingredients. Form into 1-inch balls, and place on a food dehydrator tray, leaving at least half an inch between balls. Dry at 135 degrees until firm and crisp on the outside, about 4 to 5 hours. Store in an airtight container.

Fruit Truffle

½ cup dates, chopped
½ cup dried apples, chopped
¼ cup dried cherries, chopped
¼ cup dried peaches, chopped
¼ cup golden raisins
¼ cup dried blueberries
¼ cup coconut flakes
2 tablespoons corn syrup or honey

Place all ingredients in a food processor and blend until a paste is formed. Shape into 1-inch balls. Cover and refrigerate for about an hour. Roll balls in powdered sugar, cocoa, or finely chopped nuts.

Ricotta Cream Dessert

1 ½ cups ricotta cheese
⅓ cup honey or sugar
½ teaspoon vanilla extract
1 8-ounce package cream cheese

Ginger Fruit Mix
1 cup blackberries
⅔ cup mandarin oranges
½ cup pineapple chunks
¼ cup orange juice
3 tablespoons honey
¼ teaspoon ground ginger

Place the ricotta cheese, honey, vanilla, and cream cheese in a food processor, and process until smooth.

Mix together the ginger fruit ingredients. Cover and refrigerate for an hour or until chilled.

Spoon the ricotta cheese mixture into six dessert dishes, and top with the ginger fruit mix. Serve.

Prunes & Kumquats Combo

1 cup pitted prunes
1 tablespoon sugar
¼ cup orange juice
¼ cup pineapple juice
6 kumquats, unpeeled and sliced

Cover prunes with cold water, and soak overnight. The next morning, simmer in same water until tender and plump. Remove prunes from juice. In a small saucepan, combine sugar, orange and pineapple juice, and ⅓ cup of the cooking juice from the prunes. Add the kumquats. Simmer about 5 minutes before adding the prunes. Stir to combine fruits. Serve hot or cold.

This is a nice and unusual treat.

Frozen Fruit Freeze

1 cup vanilla yogurt
½ cup spreadable fruit, any flavor
1 8-ounce package cream cheese

Line an 8-inch square pan with plastic wrap. Place all ingredients in food processor. Cover and blend until smooth. Spread in pan. Freeze for 2 hours or until firm. Remove from pan, using plastic wrap to lift. Cut into squares.

Cinnamon Orange Sauce

2 tablespoons orange marmalade
½ teaspoon ground cinnamon
½ cup plain yogurt

In a small bowl, mix together marmalade and cinnamon. Microwave for 20 seconds or more until liquefied. Let stand for 30 seconds. Stir in yogurt, mixing well. Serve with pound cake, bagels, waffles, or pancakes.

Grilled Fruit with Glaze

⅓ cup orange juice

⅔ cup brown sugar

¼ teaspoon ground cinnamon

4 cups fruit (peaches, apples, pineapples, plums, or pears), cut into 1 ½-inch pieces

Vanilla Yogurt with Ginger and Mint
1 8-ounce container vanilla yogurt

¼ teaspoon ground ginger

1 tablespoon fresh mint, chopped

Combine the ingredients for the vanilla yogurt, and chill for 30 minutes.

Combine the juice, sugar, and cinnamon in a small saucepan over medium heat. Stir until the sugar dissolves. Alternate the fruits on six 12-inch metal skewers. Prepare the grill. Brush the fruit with the glaze, and place on the grill for about 3 minutes on each sides or until slightly brown at the edges. Serve with the vanilla yogurt.

Melon Ring

2 envelopes unflavored gelatin

2 cups cold water

⅔ cup sugar

1 cup orange juice

¼ cup lemon juice

⅓ cup pineapple juice

2 cups cubed cantaloupe or honeydew

1 cup seedless green grapes

In a medium saucepan, sprinkle gelatin over cold water. Add sugar, place over low heat, and stir until gelatin is dissolved. Remove from heat. Add orange, lemon, and pineapple juice. Chill until mixture starts to jell, then fold in melon and grapes. Pour into a 6-cup ring mold, and chill until firm. Once firm, unmold, and garnish as desired.

Fruit Candy Loaf

½ cup honey
1 cup milk
½ cup chopped dates
½ cup chopped golden raisins
½ cup chopped pecans
½ cup chopped walnuts
1 teaspoon vanilla extract
1 tablespoon butter

Cook honey and milk until mixture forms a soft ball when dropped into cold water. Add fruits and nuts, and cook until mixture forms a ball. Remove from heat. Add vanilla extract and butter. Stir vigorously until stiff. Form into two 2-inch rolls, and roll in a wet cloth. Cool and store in an airtight container. Slice to serve.

Fruit Trio with Topping

2 cups diced strawberries
2 cups blueberries
2 cups kiwi
Whipped ricotta topping

Whipped Ricotta Topping
¼ cup apple juice
¼ cup sugar
1 envelope unflavored gelatin
1 cup ricotta cheese
1 cup buttermilk
1 teaspoon vanilla extract

Cook apple juice, sugar, and gelatin over medium heat for about 2 minutes, stirring occasionally, until gelatin is dissolved. Place gelatin mixture and remaining ingredients in blender. Cover and blend for about 30 seconds or until smooth. Cover and refrigerate for 30 minutes or until almost set.

Mix the strawberries, blueberries, and kiwi together. Spoon into individual dessert glasses, and top with whipped ricotta topping.

Papaya Dreamer

3 papayas
$1/2$ lime
2 tablespoons orange juice
1 cup whipped topping
1 kiwi, peeled and sliced

Cut papaya lengthwise into halves; remove seeds. Peel papaya halves. Cut papaya halves lengthwise into slices. Arrange papaya slices on four dessert plates, saving a few pieces. Squeeze lime juice over slices. Cut remaining papaya into 1-inch pieces. Place papaya pieces and orange juice in food processor. Process until smooth. Fold mixture into whipped topping. Spoon whipped topping mixture over papaya slices, and top with kiwi slices.

Pear Supreme

$3/4$ cup honey or sugar
1 1-inch piece vanilla bean
2 cups water
6 pears
1 pint vanilla bean ice cream
$2/3$ cup chocolate sauce

Combine honey, vanilla bean, and water, and bring to a boil for 5 minutes. Halve, peel, and core the pears. Poach in the syrup until tender; do not overcook. Allow pears to cool in syrup, then drain and chill. When ready to serve, place one scoop of ice cream in the bottom of individual dessert dishes, place a pear half on the ice cream, and top with a tablespoon of chocolate sauce.

Peachy Dreams

6 large ripe peaches, peeled and pitted
1/4 cup water
2 to 4 tablespoons sugar
1/8 teaspoon ground ginger
1 cup sour cream
1/2 cup chopped nuts

Peel peaches and remove pits. In a wide shallow saucepan, combine water, honey, and ginger. Heat and stir until well mixed. Then add peaches and poach gently for about 5 minutes or until peaches are soft, but not mushy. Cool the peaches, and then chill. When ready to serve, arrange two peach halves on each dessert plate, spoon the juice over each half, and then fill the center with sour cream. Sprinkle with nuts.

Peach Streusel

8 small peaches, halved
1/2 cup chopped pecans
2 tablespoons molasses
2 teaspoons butter
2 teaspoons unbleached all-purpose flour

Arrange peaches, hollow side up, on a baking sheet. Combine pecans, molasses, butter, and flour in a small bowl until well mixed. Spoon pecan mixture into the peach hollows. Press the mixture in, and then smooth out the top. Broil on the top rack of the oven until topping is bubbly, about 4 minutes. Cool to room temperature before serving.

Peach Treat with Sauce

1 cup vanilla or peach yogurt
²/₃ cup peach spreadable fruit
1 8-ounce package cream cheese
1 tablespoon sugar, more or less to taste

Raspberry Sauce
2 10-ounce packages frozen raspberries
¼ cup sugar, more or less to taste
2 teaspoons cornstarch
¼ cup water

Line an 8-inch square pan with plastic wrap. Place all ingredients in a food processor. Cover and blend, stopping to scrap sides occasionally, until smooth. Spread mixture out in pan. Freeze for about 2 hours or until firm.

To make the raspberry sauce, in a small saucepan, combine berries and sugar. Stir over low heat until just below boiling. Mix together the cornstarch and water, and add to the berries. Cook slowly until thick and smooth. Strain through a sieve. Cool. Place in a covered dish, and store in the refrigerator.

When the peach treat is frozen, remove from the pan by using the plastic wrap to lift. Cut into squares, and serve with the raspberry sauce.

We invite you to view the complete
selection of titles we publish at:

www.TEACHServices.com

Scan with your mobile
device to go directly
to our website.

Please write or email us your praises, reactions, or
thoughts about this or any other book we publish at:

P.O. Box 954
Ringgold, GA 30736

info@TEACHServices.com

TEACH Services, Inc., titles may be purchased in bulk for
educational, business, fund-raising, or sales promotional use.
For information, please e-mail:

BulkSales@TEACHServices.com

Finally, if you are interested in seeing
your own book in print, please contact us at

publishing@TEACHServices.com

We would be happy to review your manuscript for free.

www.ingramcontent.com/pod-product-compliance
Lightning Source LLC
Chambersburg PA
CBHW081841170426
43199CB00017B/2811